THE UNOFFICIAL

HARRY POTTER

JOKE BOOK

HOWLING HILARITY FOR HUFFLEPUFF

THE UNOFFICIAL
HARRY POTTER
JOKE BOOK

HOWLING HILARITY
FOR HUFFLEPUFF

BRIAN BOONE

ILLUSTRATIONS BY

AMANDA BRACK

Sky Pony Press
New York

Copyright © 2019 by Hollan Publishing, Inc.

Sky Pony Press books may be purchased in bulk at special discounts for sales promotion, corporate gifts, fund-raising, or educational purposes. Special editions can also be created to specifications. For details, contact the Special Sales Department, Sky Pony Press, 307 West 36th Street, 11th Floor, New York, NY 10018 or info@skyhorsepublishing.com.

Sky Pony® is a registered trademark of Skyhorse Publishing, Inc.®, a Delaware corporation.

Visit our website at www.skyponypress.com.

10 9 8 7 6 5 4 3 2 1

Library of Congress Cataloging-in-Publication Data is available on file.

Cover artwork by Amanda Brack and iStockphoto/Shutterstock

Paperback ISBN: 978-1-5107-4093-8
Ebook ISBN: 978-1-5107-4095-2

Printed in the United States of America

CONTENTS

Introduction

Gryffindors are brave, Slytherins are calculating, Ravenclaws are brainy . . . but what about Hufflepuffs? It's the Hogwarts house that gets the least attention in the Harry Potter books and movies, but that doesn't make its students and members any less important. They just don't get up to the same level of hijinks or drama as the wizards and witches in those other Hogwarts houses.

So yeah, Hufflepuffs may have never come close to winning a House Cup, but they're totally cool with it—that's just how Hufflepuffs roll. That easygoing nature is what defines a Hufflepuff, along with being friendly, calm, generous, inclusive, sportsman-like, nature-loving, and loyal. They do their own thing and they have a blast doing it.

Hufflepuffs *love* jokes and making their friends laugh, so for Hufflepuffs (and those who want to be Hufflepuffs), we present you with *The Unofficial Harry Potter Joke Book: Howling Hilarity for Hufflepuffs,* the fourth book in our gut-busting series of hilarity for proud Potterheads! You'll want to proudly wave the black-and-yellow with these jokes about being a Hufflepuff, life at Hogwarts as a Hufflepuff, the Hufflepuff common room, and famous Hufflepuffs like Newt Scamander, Nymphadora Tonks, and Cedric Diggory.

Don't worry, non-Hufflepuffs—there are jokes, riddles, games, and silliness galore covering all aspects of the wizarding world! So, without further ado . . . *accio jokes!*

Chapter 1

Q. What's a Hufflepuff's favorite holiday?
A. Earth Day.

•

Q. How is a Hufflepuff like a weed?
A. They bloom where they're planted.

•

Q. How else is a Hufflepuff like a weed?
A. They hang around plants a lot.

•

Q. What house produces the most doctors?
A. Hufflepuff, because they treasure patients.

The Hufflepuff points hourglass is full of yellow diamonds, or rather time-unds.

•

Q. What do you call a Hufflepuff who golfs?
A. A Hufflepuffer duffer.

•

Q. What does the Hufflepuff basement look like?
A. If you're not a Hufflepuff, you'll never know, and if you're a Hufflepuff, you'll never tell!

•

Q. What house are French-speaking kids placed in?
A. Huff Le Puff.

•

Hufflepuff bumper sticker: "Everyday I'm Hufflepuffing."

•

Q. What's the most rough-and-tumble house at Hogwarts?
A. Tough-le-puff.

For Hufflepuffs Only! (And Everybody Else)

Q. How do Hufflepuffs stay warm in the winter?
A. Earmufflepuffs.

Q. What's Helga Hufflepuff's favorite song?
A. "Cups."

Q. What house would a Pokemon get inserted into?
A. Jigglyhufflepuff.

Q. What's black, yellow, and buzzes?

A. A Hufflepuff bee.

Q. What kind of dishes do Hufflepuffs use?

A. Earthenware.

•

Q. What do you call a Slytherin with a heart?

A. A Hufflepuff.

•

Q. What do you call someone who never loses their wallet?

A. A Hufflepuff!

For Hufflepuffs Only! (And Everybody Else)

Q. What's a Hufflepuff's favorite game?

A. Hide and Seek . . . because they always win!

•

Q. Did you hear about the highly accomplished Hufflepuff?

A. Probably not, because they were too shy to brag about their achievements.

•

You know you're a Hufflepuff when . . .

- You make friends everywhere you go . . . even if you don't mean to.
- You don't like conflicts or fighting, but you're really good at sports anyway.
- People are always asking you to find things for them.
- You always find yourself dressed like a bee.
- You're glad Hufflepuff doesn't win the House Cup because you wouldn't want the other houses to get disappointed.
- You can't think of any Hufflepuff stereotypes . . . because there aren't any!
- You remind everybody that no dark wizards were Hufflepuffs.

- You wonder why people think Hufflepuffs are boring when Cedric Diggory and Tonks were Hufflepuffs.
- When reading *Goblet of Fire*, you rooted for Cedric, not Harry.
- Well, to be honest, you rooted for Cedric *and* Harry.
- You will explain what it means to be a Hufflepuff, which is the most Hufflepuff thing ever.
- When you tell your friends you're a Hufflepuff, they say, "of course you are!"

●

Q. What's a Hufflepuff's favorite thing to bake?
A. Dirt Cake.

●

Q. What's a Hufflepuff's other favorite thing to bake?
A. Mud Pie!

●

Q. How does the Fat Friar wash his hair?
A. With Shambooooo!

For Hufflepuffs Only! (And Everybody Else)

Q. How does the Fat Friar start his morning?
A. With a cup of coff-eek!

•

Q. How does a Hufflepuff make a hole?
A. They dig-gory it.

•

Q. Is Nagini a Hufflepuff?
A. She does hug people . . . to death, but still, she's a hugger.

•

Q. Why did the Hufflepuff charm her hair blonde?
A. To match her robes.

•

Q. What happened when the Hufflepuff house ghost met an Erumpent?
A. He became the Flat Friar.

•

Q. What do you call a Hufflepuff wearing their house colors while practicing charms?
A. A spelling bee!

Q. What happened when Mrs. Norris took over for the Hufflepuff house ghost?

A. She became the Cat Friar.

Q. What happened when Scabbers took over for the Hufflepuff house ghost?

A. He became the Rat Friar.

•

Q. Why is it annoying when a Hufflepuff asks for a favor?

A. Because they "badger" you.

For Hufflepuffs Only! (And Everybody Else)

Q. **What do you call a strong Hufflepuff?**
A. A Huffletough.

Q. **What Hogwarts house would Big Bird's best friend be in?**
A. Snufflehufflepuff.

Q. **Where do they put sick kids at Hogwarts?**
A. Snifflepuff.

Q. Where do they put the tough and rebellious kids at Hogwarts?

A. Hufflepunk.

Q. What's a Hufflepuff's favorite rap song?

A. "Black and Yellow."

Q. Why did Tonks think it was gross to eat with Lupin?

A. He always "wolfed" down his food!

For Hufflepuffs Only! (And Everybody Else)

Q. What's another name for the Hufflepuff crest?
A. A badger badge.

Q. Did you hear about the Slytherin who tried to enter the Hufflepuff common room?
A. They really had him over a barrel!

•

Q. How do Hufflepuffs take their sandwiches?
A. With Sprouts!

•

Q. Where does Professor Sprout send dying flowers?
A. To the hos-petal.

Q. How does a Hufflepuff make moss grow?
A. Expelliar-moss!

•

Student: Are you gonna put me in Hufflepuff? Huh, huh, are you?
Sorting Hat: Quit badgering me!

•

Q. Where did the Sorting Hat place the dog wizard?
A. Rufflepuff!

•

Q. What do you call a magical seabird?
A. A Hufflepuffin.

•

Q. How do Hufflepuffs blow up their cheeks?
A. They hufflepuff up!

•

Q. If a liar went to Hogwarts, what house would they enter?
A. Blufflepuff.

For Hufflepuffs Only! (And Everybody Else)

Q. What kind of chips do Hufflepuffs eat?
A. Huffleruffles.

Q. How do Hufflepuffs snuggle?
A. With Hugglepuffs.

Q. What house has the shiniest common room?
A. Bufflepuff!

Q. What house produces the most police officers?
A. Handcufflepuff.

Q. What do you call an underwater Hufflepuff?

A. A hufflepufferfish.

Q. How do Hufflepuffs stay informed about magical events?

A. They watch the evening Newts.

Q. Cedric told his Triwizard egg a riddle.

A. Then it cracked up.

Q. Where would you find a boggart?

A. In the boggarden!

For Hufflepuffs Only! (And Everybody Else)

Q. What house is perfect for magical peacocks?
A. Rufflepuffs.

Professor Sprout: Did you know about the student who listened to a Mandrake?
Neville: What a terrible thing to hear!

•

At first the students didn't like the Herbology class, but then they grew to enjoy it.

Neville did very well in Herbology.
Professor Sprout thinks he's a budding genius!

•

Q. What's a Hufflepuff's favorite NBA team?
A. The Boston Cedrics.

•

Q. Did you hear about Cedric and Moaning Myrtle?
A. They're dating now.

•

Cedric was a seeker, so you'd think he would have found the
Triwizard Cup right away.

•

Q. What happened when Cho broke up with her boyfriend?
A. He got Sad-ric.

•

The Fat Friar knocked over a painting. Talk about a boo-boo.

•

Q. What subject do all Hufflepuffs get an "A" in?
A. Spelling!

For Hufflepuffs Only! (And Everybody Else)

Cedric Diggory may have successfully competed in the Triwizard Tournament, but soon after, it turned into a Crywizard Tournament.

●

Q. What does the Fat Friar eat for dinner?
A. Spook-ghetti.

●

Q. Why isn't the Fat Friar allowed to go to classes?
A. The professors say he spooks out of turn.

●

Q. What does a Hufflepuff call "the boy who lived"?
A. Harry . . . something . . . the guy in Gryffindor or something.

●

Q. In what house does the Sorting Hat place the most excitable witches and wizards?
A. Kerfufflepuff!

●

Q. Why did Cedric go to study in the Great Lake?
A. Because he was "swamped" with homework!

Chapter 2

Q. What do Professor Snape and Professor McGonagall have in common?

A. The same first name . . . Professor!

•

Q. What's as big as the *Hogwarts Express* but doesn't weigh anything?

A. The *Hogwarts Express*'s shadow.

•

Q. How did the conductor learn how to drive the *Hogwarts Express*?

A. Training!

•

Q. What goes up and down but doesn't move?

A. A Hogwarts spiral staircase.

Q. What has forty feet and sings?
A. The Hogwarts choir.

•

Q. When is a door not a door?
A. When it's a Dumbledore.

•

Ron: Someone said you sound like Hedwig.
Harry: Who?

•

Q. Who's the best at managing mischief?
A. A mischief manager.

•

Q. Who's second-best at managing mischief?
A. An assistant mischief manager.

•

Hermione was so appalled by the treatment of house elves, it made her want to SPEW!

Q. How do Dumbles get into Hogwarts?

A. Through the Dumblewindow. Just kidding, they use the Dumbledore.

•

Q. What did Moaning Myrtle get on Valentine's Day?

A. A boo-quet!

•

Q. Why don't the house ghosts fight?

A. They haven't got the guts.

•

Q. How did the Hogwarts student get high marks?

A. With a ladder and a pencil.

•

Q. What do you call a wizard who failed all his OWLs?

A. Not a future Hogwarts professor.

•

Q. Did you hear that Hedwig got laryngitis?

A. She didn't give a hoot!

Around Hogwarts

Q. Did you know all the Hogwarts students sleep in huge rooms?

A. Some people think that's a dorm idea.

•

Q. Why can't students write with a broken quill?

A. It's pointless.

Q. What's the difference between a fast food kitchen and a Hogwarts ghost?

A. One is a fat fryer and the other is the Fat Friar.

Q. What are air, food, and water to Hermione?
A. Hermioneeds.

●

Q. In what house would you find students who wear wooden shoes?
A. Ravenclog!

Q. Did you hear about the dog that stumbled across Hogwarts?
A. She went from wags to witches.

Q. If centaurs went to Hogwarts, into what house would they be sorted?

A. Ravenclop.

•

Draco is so annoying.

He's always trying to Slytherin to other people's conversations.

•

Harry: How was school this term, James?

James: Professor McGonnagall told me to stop goofing off and to be more serious.

Harry: Oh yeah?

James: I told her it would be easy, because "Sirius" is my middle name.

•

Q. What do you call it when you're hanging around with Lupin?

A. A here-wolf!

•

Q. What do you call Hagrid's dog when it's sleeping?

A. A snorehound.

Q. When does a worm have a tail?

A. When it's Wormtail.

•

Q. Who always took notes for the Marauder's Map crew?

A. Pad-foot!

•

One time, the Marauders got caught pulling a prank and received detention.

"Oh deer," said James.

"Oh, rats," said Peter.

"Doggone it!" said Sirius.

•

Q. What's the difference between a cranky house elf and Professor Sprout?

A. One's Kreacher, and one's a teacher!

•

That Triwizard Tournament took forever.

It just kept dragon on.

Q. When does the Sorting Hat reject you from all four houses?

A. When you put the Sorting Hat on your feet!

Q. Why did Hermione bring a Visa card to her professor?

A. For extra credit.

Q. What does Peeves make for dessert?

A. Boo-berry crumble.

Q. Did you hear that Hogwarts hired a vampire to be the Defense Against the Dark Arts instructor?

A. Her tests were terrible—they were blood tests!

•

Q. How come the Inferi never came to their classes?

A. They were always feeling so rotten.

•

Q. When did Sirius do well in school?

A. When there was a pup quiz!

•

Q. What happens if you cross Hermione with Peter Pettigrew?

A. A bookwormtail!

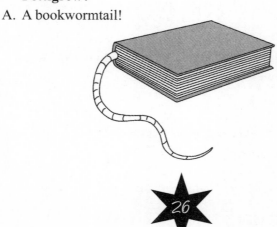

Q. How is a Hogwarts classroom like an acromantula?
A. Too many pupils!

●

Q. Did you know that Hermione's parents are dentists?
A. Well, Granger things have happened.

●

Q. What do Ravenclaws eat at barbecues?
A. Ravenslaw.

●

Q. How do you find the bathroom at Hogwarts?
A. You use Loo Powder.

●

Q. What house ghost used to be a vampire hunter?
A. The Bat Fryer.

●

Q. Did you know there's a cap store at Hogwarts?
A. It's guarded by the Hat Lady.

Q. Did you hear a wizard got mad and turned a nosy reporter into bread?

A. Now she's Pita Skeeter.

●

Q. What house do zombies belong to?

A. Witherin.

Q. What do you get when you cross Crookshanks with McGonagall?

A. Exasperated kittens.

Q. What do you get when you cross a fish with a loopy witch?

A. Tuna Lovegood.

•

Q. Did you hear about Professor Trelawney's ugly handbag?

A. It was an unforgivable purse!

•

Q. What Hogwarts staffer is in charge of dogs?

A. Madame Pooch.

•

Q. What do sorcerers eat with their tea?

A. Sorcerer's scones!

•

Q. Did you hear that Draco turned Harry into a potato?

A. Now he's Harry Totter.

•

Q. What do you get when you cross a Ravenclaw with the sick bay?

A. Ill-literacy

Q. How do you get into the Hogwarts gym?

A. You just use the dumbbell door.

●

Q. The house ghosts formed a little choir.

A. They always sang such haunting melodies.

●

Q. What do house ghosts like to chew?

A. Boo-bble gum!

Q. Did you hear that Hermione couldn't turn in her ancient symbols homework?

A. It was in runes!

Q. What makes Hogwarts so unique?
A. It's the only school where kids can curse in class!

•

Q. Which house ghost is the dirtiest?
A. The Muddy Baron.

Q. What's the most unrealistic thing about the Harry Potter books?
A. That someone like Draco has two friends.

•

Q. What do you get if you crossed Hermione with Professor Sprout's class?
A. Herb-ione!

Q. What ghost is always in a bad mood?
A. The Moody Baron.

●

Q. What Hogwarts club is just okay?
A. The Shrug Club.

●

Q. What goblin works in the Hogwarts library?
A. Gripbook.

●

Q. Why did Dumbledore cross the road?
A. He was following the trail of lemon drops.

●

When the Patil twins trade places, that's what's known as a "s-witch"!

●

As a boy, Professor Dumbledore was a regular "wiz" kid.

●

Q. Why did the Gray Lady go to the dentist?
A. For a crown.

When Hagrid got that baby dragon, it sure was egg-cellent.

Nearly Headless Nick nearly lost his head.
It was a terrible ax-ident.

•

Q. Why did Professor Flitwick like third year students the best?

A. Because the third time's the charm!

•

Q. Did you hear about the Slytherin who didn't get anything fun for Christmas because he was bad?

A. They called him Draco No-Toy.

Kids in Charms class were asked to be seated.
They had to sit for a spell.

•

Q. What does Professor Flitwick eat for breakfast?
A. Lucky Charms.

•

Q. Does Snape love Hedwig, after all this time?
A. Owlways!

•

Q. Ron hated doing his chores.
A. He'd always Weasley his way out of them.

•

Professor Sprout has all the good gossip.
She hears about it through the grapevine.

•

Professor Lupin always paid close attention.
They called him "aware wolf."

Professor Flitwick makes sure there's no cheating in his classes. He always runs a spell check.

●

Q. What do you call a non-magical person who sneaks into Hogwarts?
A. A smuggled muggle!

●

The tall birds never wanted to hang out with Hagrid. He'd been ostrich-sized.

●

Q. Who's the loudest student at Hogwarts?
A. Katie Bell.

●

Q. Where does Harry's godfather hear all the good new music?
A. Sirius Radio.

●

Q. Why did Snape cross the road twice?
A. Because he's a double-crosser.

35

Ron always stood on Harry's left-hand side. That way no matter where he chose to go, it was a matter of right and Ron.

•

Hermione always returned her library books on time. Otherwise, the Hogwarts librarian would give her a "pince" of her mind!

•

Q. What do a popular wizard band and a pair of Gryffindor twins have in common?

A. They're all "weird sisters"!

•

Q. Where did Hermione find Crookshanks?

A. In a cat-alog.

•

Q. Why aren't there any sharks in the lake around Hogwarts?

A. The Dementors scared them away.

Around Hogwarts

Q. Where do sick Slytherins seek treatment?

A. At a hiss-pital.

•

Q. On what day does Mrs. Norris relax?

A. Cat-urday!

•

Whenever Lupin turned into a werewolf, he'd have to put his life on "paws."

•

Q. Was Lupin a good werewolf?

A. Sure, he was a howling success!

•

Nearly Headless Nick wasn't sure what he was going to do when he became a ghost. But then he pulled himself together.

•

Q. Why couldn't Harry find his invisibility cloak?

A. Because it's invisible.

Q. What do Marauders do after using the Marauder's Map?

A. They take a Marauder's nap.

•

Ron: I can't do this homework on an empty stomach.
Harry: You should probably do it on paper.

•

Q. How can you tell Fred and George apart?

A. Fred is probably the one who will tell you he's George, and George is the one who will say his name is Fred.

•

Q. Why did Hermione buy two copies of the same book?

A. To read it twice to prepare for the test.

•

Ginny: I've got six brothers.
Hufflepuff student: I wish I had six brothers.
Ginny: Don't you have any brothers?
Hufflepuff student: Yes, I've got twelve!

Q. What's the weather at Hogwarts like?
A. Too foggy to tell.

•

Professor Snape: I invented a potion to make you travel through walls.
Professor McGonagall: Neat. I'll use this door.

•

Attending Potions class is a stirring experience.

•

For so many young magical people, getting to attend Hogwarts is a witch come true.

•

Q. What kind of knives do the cooks at Hogwarts use?
A. Witchblades.

•

Q. How can you tell a Dementor is near?
A. There's a dread giveaway.

Q. Who makes the gravy in the Hogwarts kitchen?
A. The saucerer.

•

Harry: Did you read the book about the giant's forehead?
Hermione: No, it's too highbrow.

•

Cho: Why don't you want to talk about your godfather, Harry?
Harry: I don't feel like answering any Sirius questions.

•

Q. What's the first thing a wizard reads after graduating from Hogwarts?
A. The "Help Wanted" ads.

•

Q. Why did Professor Flitwick run the Hogwarts choir?
A. He always gave very sound instruction.

•

Q. Who didn't get invited to the Hogwarts class reunion?
A. Voldemort.

Q. Did you hear about the Hogwarts prom?

A. It was a magical evening!

•

Madame Pomfrey was such a kind staff member.
She always had the most patients!

•

Q. Hogwarts didn't pay the cleaning bills for its living paintings.

A. They were nearly re-possessed!

•

Q. What do you get when you cross math with a Care of Magical Creatures class?

A. Owl-gebra!

•

Q. Did you hear that were going to make an entire book about Harry's godfather?

A. They canceled it because they thought it would be too Sirius.

Hedwig: Who!
Hermione: Whom.

•

Mrs. Norris was a valuable part of the Hogwarts staff. She had a certain number of tasks purr day.

•

Q. Why did Hedwig get detention at Hogwarts?
A. For using owl language.

•

Q. Why did Neville kill Nagini?
A. He's just that sword of guy.

•

The young wizard was in love with his classmate. What could he say, he was spellbound!

•

Q. What do house elves learn in school?
A. The elf-abet.

Q. What kind of treasure would you find in a shack on the Hogwarts grounds?

A. Rubeus!

•

Herbology was a popular class at Hogwarts.
Students there had the thyme of their life.

•

Q. How do wizards fix mistakes in math class?

A. "Hex-a-gone!"

•

Q. How are Harry Potter books held together?

A. They're spellbound!

•

Q. How are the potions at Hogwarts kept safe from thieves?

A. With a warlock.

•

Dolores Umbridge always hated being the centaur of attention.

43

Q. Did you hear that Filch dresses Mrs. Norris in wizard robes?

A. They're purrr-ple.

•

Q. You think Harry Potter is your best friend?

A. That's just Ron!

•

Q. What's it called when you never receive your letter to Hogwarts?

A. A muggle struggle.

•

Q. Why did James Potter not turn in his homework?

A. Because Lupin ate it.

•

Q. What's the difference between a comma and Crookshanks?

A. A comma is a pause at the end of a clause, and Crookshanks has claws at the end of his paws.

Q. What happens when you cross Hedwig with the flying instructor?

A. Madame Whooch.

•

Q. What happens when you cross Fang with the flying instructor?

A. Madame Pooch.

Q. What's the stinkiest thing at Hogwarts?

A. Those "Potter Stinks!" badges.

Chapter 3

MAGICAL PLACES AND ENCHANTED SPACES

Q. What's Harry Potter's favorite Diagon Alley store?
A. The cauldron shop, of course, because he's a potter.

•

Q. Which is the cheapest Diagon Alley store?
A. Bargain and Burkes.

•

SHOPLIFTERS WILL BE TRANSFIGURED.
—*sign in a Diagon Alley shop*

•

Two Pyromancers walk into the Leaky Cauldron. One of them says, "Is it hot in here, or is it just us?"

Q. Where can a wizard buy rulers, protractors, and graph paper?

A. Diagonal Alley.

•

Q. Where do magical robots keep their money?

A. Gringbots.

Q. Who controls sadness?

A. The Ministry of Tragic.

●

Q. Why did the Death Eaters get sent to Azkaban?

A. So the Dementors could warlock them up!

●

Q. Where would you buy flowers for Neville's parents?

A. At the Petrified Florist.

●

Q. What's the deadliest state for wizards?

A. Nevada Kadavra!

●

Q. Did you know Gringotts has a location on the water?

A. It's down by the riverbanks.

●

Dobby got sick and went to St. Mungo's.
He had pretty good elf care.

Q. How do prisoners in Azkaban communicate?
A. With cell phones.

Q. What day does Florean Fortescue's Ice Cream Parlour open?
A. Sundae.

Q. Where do Death Eaters go on vacation?
A. Hexico City.

Q. Why did Sirius shower before he escaped Azkaban?
A. He wanted to make a clean getaway.

Q. What kind of music do bad wizards listen to?
A. Jazzkaban.

•

Q. Who cleans up around the merpeople castle?
A. The mer-maid.

Harry: Are you meeting your family at King's Cross Station?
Ron: No, I've known them for years!

•

Q. What structure can protect you from dark lords?
A. De fence against de dark arts.

Magical Places and Enchanted Spaces

Q. What's the hardest village to find?
A. Fogsmeade.

Q. What do magical cheerleaders eat?
A. Exploding pompoms from Honeydukes.

Q. Where can you buy magical Legos?
A. Blockturn Alley.

Q. What's the best music store for wizards?
A. Rockturn Alley.

Q. What's the loudest tree in the forest?
A. The Clomping Willow.

Q. Where do Gringotts employees buy their candy?
A. Moneydukes.

In Hogsmeade, the parties are great because they always go
hog wild.

•

Q. Why is the Whomping Willow always whomping?
A. Just because it's so knotty!

•

**Q. Did you hear that Nagini dropped by Godric's Hollow
but nobody was there?**
A. She left her crawling card.

Q. Why did the goblin quit her job at Gringotts?
A. A knut allergy.

A witch thought about going to work at Azbakan and she made a list of reasons why and why not. She turned it down, deciding that there were too many cons.

•

Q. Where in Diagon Alley can you buy a beautiful bouquet?
A. At Flowerish & Blotts.

Q. What's the difference between Mad-Eye Moody and an owl shop?
A. One is a cyclops, and the other is Eeylops.

Q. Where in Diagon Alley can you buy an android?
A. At Flourish & Bots.

•

Q. Where in Diagon Alley can you buy a monkey?
A. Gambol & Apes.

Ron: I can tell you your favorite Diagon Alley shop, I bet.
Fred: Oh really?
Ron: Gamble and Japes, get it?

Q. Why is the Godric's Hollow graveyard so exclusive?
A. Because people are dying to get in!

•

Q. Why is there always room in Harry Potter's hometown?
A. It is "hollow!"

•

Q. What happens when you cross a carload of wizards with a swarm of bees?
A. The Knight Buzz.

•

Two Hungarian Horntails walk into the Leaky Cauldron. The first one says, "It sure is hot in here." The second one says, "Close your mouth!"

•

Q. What kind of fish do Gringotts goblins like the most?
A. Goldfish.

•

Q. How does a new Azkaban prison guard learn the ropes?
A. From their mentor Dementor.

Q. What do Dementors on the job talk about?

A. Nothing much, they mostly just Azkabanter.

Q. What kind of bug infestation would Gringotts welcome?

A. Silverfish.

Q. Did you hear about the stressful day for the Gringotts goblin?

A. It had him in knuts!

Q. What do you call a Dementor who gets fired but then gets its job back at Azkaban?

A. A Re-mentor.

•

Q. What do you call the Weasley house in the winter?

A. The Burrow, of course. That's its name!

Chapter 4

SPELLS, POTIONS, AND MAGICAL OBJECTS

Ron took that Muggle car, but he didn't know how to use it and crashed it. At the end of the day, it wasn't a car at all . . . but an error-plane.

•

Q. What do you call a blindfolded stag patronus?
A. No eye deer!

Spells, Potions, and Magical Objects

Q. How much does it cost to get a stag patronus?
A. A buck.

•

Q. Why did Harry see his father's patronus?
A. Because he was very deer to Harry.

•

Q. What color is the hair of the Hogwarts Potions Master?
A. Snape? He's a "brew"-net!

•

Q. What spell does Moaning Myrtle use the most?
A. Loo-mos!

•

Don't eat a Time-Turner.
It's very time-consuming.

•

Q. What do the cooks in the Hogwarts kitchen use when they're running late on a meal?
A. A Thyme-Turner.

Q. How do wizards transform into parrots?
A. With Polly-Juice Potion.

Q. How do you make an enchanted boat work?
A. A portkey!

Q. What's the difference between a shady wizard and a charm that leads to confusion?
A. One is Mundungus and the other is a Confundus!

Q. Have you ever seen Harry Potter's patronus?
A. It's staggering!

•

Q. Did you hear about the wizard's plan to freeze Liquid Luck and use it later?
A. It was pretty solid.

•

Q. How could Molly Weasley make so many sweaters so fast?
A. She just used a loom-os spell.

Q. What happened to the broken-down truck full of chocolate frogs?

A. It got toad.

•

Q. How do chocolate frogs avoid getting eaten?

A. An invisibility croak.

•

Q. Where do they find those chocolate frogs anyway?

A. Chocolate bogs.

•

Q. What's black and white and red all over?

A. A Howler in a tuxedo.

•

Q. How do wizard dentists treat cavities?

A. A Filling Curse.

•

Q. Why didn't Lupin wear a watch?

A. He didn't want to get ticks.

Q. What potion will turn you into Santa?
A. Holly Juice Potion.

Q. What kind of magic can you use to revive a Tyrannosaurus Rex?
A. Dino-sorcery.

Q. How do chocolate frogs greet each other?
A. "Warts up?"

Q. How does a wizard make a dog go away?
A. Expelliarmutt!

•

Q. How do you heal bruised fruit?
A. Re-pear-o!

•

Q. How do you start a magical party?
A. Accio rumpus!

•

Q. What do shapeshifters put on their walls?
A. Bogg-art.

•

Q. How do you make enough water for everyone?
A. Aguaplenty!

•

Q. Where did Ron fill up his magical car?
A. At the Fueling Club.

Q. Why did Amelia Bones order lobsters?

A. She was head of the Department of Magical Claw Enforcement.

•

Q. How do you heal an injured bird?

A. Reparrot!

Q. How do you get your friend to stop playing terrible music?

A. Expelliarmusic!

Q. Wizard doctors only accept payment in knuts and galleons.

A. They don't care for sickles.

•

Q. How do you turn a chicken into a cow?

A. A Farm Charm.

•

Q. What do you call a magical object that reminded you of boxing matches you'd seen?

A. A remembrawl.

•

Q. How do wizards know what's on TV?

A. Tivination.

•

Q. How come the baseball cap didn't make a good Sorting Hat?

A. There was no point.

Spells, Potions, and Magical Objects

Q. Did you hear about the yellow spell caster?
A. It was a blonde wand.

•

Q. How can a short wizard gain height?
A. A Tally Juice Potion.

•

Q. How can a wizard protect their porch?
A. A welcome mat-ronus.

•

Q. What's an animal projection of Mr. Weasley?
A. A Pa-Ron-us.

•

Q. Did you hear Bertie Bott made vegetables?
A. They're called "Every Flavor Greens"!

•

Q. Who can fix a magical sailboat?
A. The Potions mast-er.

Q. What do wizards bring out at Fourth of July parties?

A. The Goblet of Fireworks.

Q. What magical object makes you waste time?

A. The Time-Burner.

Q. How do you get a cow patronus?

A. A summoning farm.

Spells, Potions, and Magical Objects

Q. Why wasn't Horace Slughorn a good driver?
A. Because he'd always turn into an armchair.

•

Q. Why did Harry give away his invisibility cloak?
A. He just couldn't see himself wearing it.

•

Q. What do you call a malfunctioning Remembrall?
A. A Remembralmost!

•

Q. How do you make a Remembrall work?
A. Feed it a Remembralmond!

•

Q. What do wizards call a clock?
A. A broken Time-Turner.

•

Q. What do wizards call mail?
A. Quiet Howlers.

Q. Did you hear what happened when Crookshanks wandered inside the Sorting Hat?

A. Dr. Seuss wrote a book about it called *The Cat in the Hat*.

•

Little wizards play with little dolls that they can turn into anything else.

They're action transfigures.

•

Q. How do you make a chicken skewer appear?

A. Avada Kebabra!

•

Q. How do you make your friend Barbara appear?

A. Avada Ka-Barbara!

•

Q. Did you hear about the great honor bestowed on the Goblet of Fire?

A. It's going into the Hall of Flame!

Don't take the Goblet of Fire seriously.
It makes light of everything.

•

Q. The Goblet of Fire wasn't always good at its job.
A. It was once torch and go.

•

Q. Where did Dumbledore first find the Goblet of Fire?
A. At a fire sale.

•

Even though Harry Potter knew how to use gillyweed,
sometimes his grades were below C-level.

•

Q. How do bakers get selected to work in the Hogwarts kitchen?
A. The Shortening Hat.

•

Q. What kind of magic hurts the most?
A. Sore-cery.

Draco: I'll have you know that my wand is worth more than 1,000 galleons!

Luna: What kind of job did it have to earn that much?

•

Q. Where did Godric Gryffindor find his sword?

A. In the Swording Hat.

Q. Did you hear about the android appointed Minister of Magic?

A. It's Kingsley Shackle-Bot!

What Wizards Call Common Things

- Stick – dog magic wand
- Garden hose – water wand
- Pool cue – Game wand
- Baseball bat – Quidditch wand
- Paint brush – art wand
- Pen – homework wand
- Fork – food wand
- Remote control – TV wand
- Hammer – garage wand
- Weedwhacker – yard wand
- Long-stemmed rose – love wand
- Walrus tusk – ocean wand
- Arm – human wand
- Curling iron – hair wand
- Skewer – barbecue wand
- Sword – fencing wand
- Knife – cutting wand
- Tennis racket – court wand
- Toothbrush - dental wand

●

Q. What's another name for the Pensieve?
A. The Wizarding Whirrled!

Q. How do you "do the hippogriff," anyway?

A. It's all in the hips.

●

Q. What spell must you use to conjure a magical animal that's just okay?

A. Accepto patronum.

●

Q. How many wizards does it take to change a light bulb?

A. Wizards don't use light bulbs.

Chapter 5

FANTASTIC BEASTS (AND HERE IS WHERE YOU'LL FIND THEM)

Q. What do you get from an angry Erumpent?
A. As far away as possible!

•

Q. How can you tell when an Erumpent will charge?
A. He takes out his credit card.

•

Q. Which side of a Fwooper has the most feathers?
A. The outside.

•

Q. What did the Niffler say to Newt?
A. Nothing—Nifflers can't talk.

Q. What do you call a centaur wearing earmuffs?

A. Anything you want—he can't hear you.

Q. What do you call an Erumpent that makes a lot of mistakes?

A. An error-umpent.

Q. How do you rid a place of Blast-End Skrewts?

A. With a Blast-End Skrewt-driver.

Q. How do you learn to style a hippogriff?
A. A Hair of Magical Creatures class.

Q. What's black, fluffy, and silences a car?
A. A Nuffler.

Q. What magical creatures will fix up your yard?
A. Mowtruckles.

Q. What do you call a werewolf who lives in a barn?
A. Fenrir Hayback.

Q. How do you make a horse immortal?
A. With the Horserer's Stone.

•

Q. What do you call an upset half-horse, half-eagle?
A. Hippomiffed.

•

Q. What do you get when you cross the Denver Broncos and the Philadelphia Eagles?
A. A hippogriff!

•

Q. Where wouldn't you find a hippo?
A. In a hippogriff's family tree.

•

Q. What magical creatures smell the best?
A. Scentaurs.

•

Q. Who puts out fires in the wizarding world?
A. Douse elves.

Fantastic Beasts (And Here is Where You'll Find Them)

Q. What doctors treat werewolf bites?
A. Cure-bloods.

•

Q. What dragon is full of cold sodas?
A. The Norwegian Fridgeback.

•

Q. The Basilisk once bit poor Crookshanks.
A. He was catatonic!

•

Q. Was Harry afraid of the basilisk?
A. Sure, he was downright petrified.

•

Q. How do you measure a basilisk?
A. In meters, because they don't have feet.

•

Q. Where do the merpeople in the Black Lake sleep?
A. On waterbeds.

Q. Why is the Giant Squid so imposing?
A. It's well-armed!

Q. How can you tell if a Giant Squid likes you?
A. They'll ink at you.

•

Q. How do you make a Giant Squid laugh?
A. Ten tickles.

Fantastic Beasts (And Here is Where You'll Find Them)

Q. What's a Giant Squid's favorite kind of sandwich?
A. A sub.

•

Q. Why did the Giant Squid cross the Great Lake?
A. To get to the other tide.

•

Q. Did you know that there are two Giant Squids in the Great Lake?
A. They're i-tentacle twins!

•

"Look at that Giant Squid!" Harry said, superficially.

•

Q. Did you hear about the centaur who almost lost his voice?
A. He was partially hoarse.

•

Q. Why did the Niffler like Newt so much?
A. It took a shine to him.

Q. How do you get a fairy to clean?

A. You say "pixie, dust!"

Q. What do Gringotts and a Niffler have in common?

A. They're both usually full of shiny coins.

•

Q. Why did the Niffler disappear?

A. It wanted to steal away.

•

Q. Where do a wizard's keys go when they lose them?

A. Into a Niffler.

Fantastic Beasts (And Here is Where You'll Find Them)

Q. When a store found out the Niffler swiped a bunch of things, what did it do?

A. They put them on his bill.

•

Q. Why didn't the Billywig want to fly around?

A. She was feeling blue.

•

Q. How did Newt know the marmite was hungry?

A. He was very transparent about it.

•

Q. What's the difference between a doctor and a Diricawl?

A. One operates, and one apparates.

•

Q. What do mooncalves grow into?

A. Mooncows.

•

Q. Why would an Acromantula make a great Hogwarts professor?

A. They already have so many pupils.

Q. What did Ron say to the Acromantula?

A. "Stop bugging me!"

●

Q. How do you know when a glow bug is excited?

A. When they're positively glowing!

●

Q. What comes before a Thunderbird?

A. A lightning bird!

A Thunderbird is really big but quite friendly, to be Frank.

•

Q. What house would a Runespoor wind up in?
A. Slytherin, Slytherin, Slytherin.

•

Q. What can a Fwooper do better than anyone?
A. Fwoop!

•

Q. What's a Bowtruckle's favorite candy?
A. Twigs!

•

Q. How do magical rodents exercise?
A. They take a Murt-lap.

•

Q. Do you like Bowtruckles?
A. They'll really stick with you.

Q. What horn should you never try to play?

A. A Graphorn!

•

Q. What's both exciting and boring?

A. Chasing an Erumpent. You may run fast, but it will probably "bore" you.

•

Q. What does a fancy Bowtruckle wear?

A. A bow tie.

Fantastic Beasts (And Here is Where You'll Find Them)

Q. How do Bowtruckles travel?

A. By the Bowtruckle load.

•

Q. Where are Erumpents found?

A. They're so big they never get lost!

•

Q. What do you get when you cross an Erumpent with a Niffler?

A. A squashed Niffler!

•

Q. What do you get when you cross an Erumpent with a fly?

A. An Erumpent on your ceiling.

•

Q. Does anyone want to pet a Nundu?

A. Most wizards have been asked if they'd like to and Nundu.

•

Q. What's the difference between a garbage barge and a Doxy?

A. One's a dark ferry and the other is a dark fairy.

Harry: Those centaurs sure are prickly.
Hermione: Perhaps it's because they don't have a stable
   environment.

•

Q. Can you name a magical creature that steals shiny things?
A. A Niffler.

Q. Can you name another one?
A. Another Niffler.

•

Hermione: Was that a Doxy?
Ron: I'm fairy certain it was.

Fantastic Beasts (And Here is Where You'll Find Them)

Q. Why do the merpeople live underwater?
A. Because they're too old to go to Hogwarts.

•

Q. What do you get when you cross a Knarl with a balloon?
A. A popped balloon!

•

Q. Why does a griffin have an eagle's head?
A. Because that's where they drew the lion.

•

Q. Have you ever been poked by a magical quilled animal?
A. It's totally Knarl-y!

•

Q. Did you hear that the acromantula saw an eye doctor?
A. It found out it has 20/20/20/20/20/20/20/20 vision!

•

Q. What has ten eyes and scares easily?
A. An acromantula and Mad-Eye Moody.

Q. Does a phoenix fly south for the winter?
A. Sure, if it can afford the plane fare.

•

Q. If you meet an angry Erumpent, what steps should you take?
A. Big and fast ones.

•

Q. What do you serve an Erumpent for dinner?
A. Erumpent roast.

•

Q. Why can't centaurs dance?
A. They have two left feet.

•

Ginny: Whenever I close my eyes, I can't stop seeing the basilisk.
Dumbledore: Have you seen anybody?
Ginny: No, just the basilisk.

Q. Why can the Erumpent handle a few insults?
A. It's got a thick skin.

●

Q. When is a crab a turtle?
A. When it's a fire crab.

Q. What do you get when you cross an eagle and a horse?
A. A hippogriff.

●

Q. What do you get when a Giant Squid moves too fast?
A. Squid marks.

Q. **Where would you find a Giant Squid that's down on its luck?**

A. Squid row.

•

Q. **Is that centaur going anywhere in particular in the Forbidden Forest?**

A. No, he's just Ronan.

•

Q. **Did you hear about the angry house elf who eased up over the years?**

A. He was quite the Kreacher.

•

Q. **Why did Newt take a Fwooper to an animal hospital?**

A. It was feeling under the feather.

•

Q. **Did you know that dragons are total snobs?**

A. The flame went to their heads!

Fantastic Beasts (And Here is Where You'll Find Them)

Q. How can you tell if there's an Erumpent in your fridge?
A. You can't get the door closed.

•

Q. How do dragons take their steaks?
A. Medium roar.

•

Q. Why is a Demiguise so interesting?
A. Why, it's transparent!

•

Q. What did the Thunderbird say to Newt?
A. "Can I be Frank with you?"

•

Q. Who's the coolest of all magical creatures?
A. A hipster-griff.

•

Q. Why did the Hungarian Horntail need work?
A. He kept getting fired.

Q. What magical creature will you most often find on the internet?

A. Trolls!

•

Q. What do you get when you cross giant, gross creatures with a bard?

A. Giant Dung Beedles.

•

Q. Why did the Niffler steal the goldfish?

A. It took a shine to it.

•

Q. Did you hear that the magical insect was feeling blue?

A. It's okay because it was a Billywig, and they're always blue.

•

Q. What time is it when a Niffler steals your wallet?

A. Time to get a new wallet.

•

Q. What do you get if you cross a cat and a Graphorn?

A. A monster that's purrrrrple.

Fantastic Beasts (And Here is Where You'll Find Them)

Q. What has two horns and is found at the South Pole?
A. A freezing cold Graphorn.

●

Q. How is Diricawl similar to a chocolate frog around Ron Weasley?
A. They'll both disappear very fast!

●

Q. Why are Bowtruckles good at gymnastics?
A. They always "stick" the landing.

●

Q. What are Bowtruckles thinking about?
A. Wooden you like to know!

●

Q. What does a Diricawl wear when he rides a motorcycle?
A. A feather jacket.

●

Q. Why does a Runespoor exist?
A. Because three heads are better than one!

Q. What do you call a chimaera with a goat's head, lion's tail, and dragon's body?

A. Not sure what that is, but it isn't a chimaera.

Q. Why are Diricawls so ticklish?

A. Because they're covered in feathers!

Q. What should you do if you find a grindylow in your pool?

A. Let it have the pool.

Fantastic Beasts (And Here is Where You'll Find Them)

Q. What kind of music does a Billywig like best?

A. The blues.

•

Q. What does it mean if your feather pillow suddenly disappears?

A. It wasn't a pillow – it was a Diricawl!

•

Q. What happens if you hear an Augurey call?

A. You're dooooooooomed!

•

Q. What did the jewelry store do after the Niffler stole half its stock?

A. They put it on its bill.

•

Q. What can hold as many Knuts as Gringotts but is a fraction of the size?

A. A Niffler.

Chapter 6

A WHOLE NEWT WORLD
(HUFFLEPUFF'S MAGIZOOLOGIST)

Q. Why did young Newt Scamander collect so many birds?
A. Because they were going cheep.

•

Q. Where does Newt buy his hamburgers?
A. Fantastic Meats and Where to Find Them.

•

Q. What instrument did Newt play in the Hogwarts band?
A. The Erumpent.

•

Q. Where does Newt buy his pants?
A. Fantastic Pleats and Where to Find Them.

•

Q. Who's Newt's favorite Sesame Street character?
A. Big Fwooper!

Q. Did you hear Newt recorded a dance music album?

A. It's called *Fantastic Beats and Where to Drop Them*.

•

Q. What do you get when you cross Newt Scamander and a goat?

A. Fantastic Bleats and Where to Find Them.

Q. Why was Newt Scamander worried about his animals?

A. Because everybody was on his case.

•

Q. What's Newt Scamander's favorite fairy tale?

A. *Beauty and the Beast*.

99

Q. What kind of laugh does Newt Scamander make?

A. He Bowchuckles.

●

Q. Who is Newt's favorite band?

A. The Dung Beetles.

●

Q. Why didn't Newt buy a new suitcase?

A. All his money was in Nifflers.

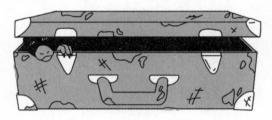

Q. What do you call Scamander's time in Hufflepuff?

A. Newt's roots.

●

Q. What's Newt Scamander's favorite old novel?

A. *The Graphorn of Notre Dame.*

A Whole Newt World (Hufflepuff's Magizoologist)

Q. What's Scamander's favorite sitcom?

A. *Newt Girl.*

•

Q. What do you get when you cross a magizoologist and a pirate?

A. Loot Scamander.

•

Q. Did Scamander discover his magizoology abilities late in life?

A. Nope, he Newt all along.

•

Q. What do you do if you want to watch *Fantastic Beasts and Where to Find Them*, but not listen to it?

A. Mute Scamander.

•

Q. What do you get when you cross a magizoologist and a cowboy?

A. Boot Scamander.

•

Q. What did the Giant Squid say when Harry told him a joke?

A. "I'm kraken up!"

Q. What do you call a magizoologist who takes up the trumpet?

A. Toot Scamander.

•

Q. What do you get when you cross a magizoologist and a kitten?

A. Cute Scamander.

Q. What would you call it if Newt hadn't survive the inquest in America?

A. A tragizoologist.

A Whole Newt World (Hufflepuff's Magizoologist)

Q. Do Scamander's owls hoot?
A. Nope, they Newt.

•

Q. Did you hear Newt Scamander opened a buffet?
A. It's called Fantastic Feasts and Where to Find Them.

•

Q. What do you call a just-hitched magizoologist?
A. A Newtly-wed.

•

Q. What mode is Newt Scamander always in?
A. Beast mode!

•

Q. Does Newt Scamander carry his magical creatures with him?
A. Yes, it's an open and shut case.

•

Q. Did you hear that Newt wrote a song for Mary Poppins?
A. "Chim-chimaera, chim-chimaera, chim-chim-cherr-ee, a lion and goat and a dragon make three!"

Chapter 7

Q. What happened to the Quidditch player who slid off their broom?

A. They fell all over themselves.

•

Q. Why are Quidditch players so admirable?

A. They achieve their goals!

The Quidditch Pitch

Q. Why was the Quidditch player angry?

A. She had a bad altitude.

•

Q. Besides the golden snitch, what do Quidditch players catch?

A. Colds!

James Potter thought using his Patronus to play Quidditch would be a great idea.

But he just wound up staggering around.

•

Q. Is the Hogwarts Quidditch pitch the best in the world?

A. Well, it's definitely up there.

Q. Why did the not-so-smart wizard try to take a Quidditch class?

A. He was interested in higher education.

•

The Beater didn't know why the ball kept getting bigger. Then it hit him.

Q. Why can't Quidditch players tell each other secrets?

A. Because of the snitch.

The Quidditch Pitch

Q. What do new Quidditch players do for energy?
A. They have launch!

●

Q. Who cleans up the stadium after a Quidditch match?
A. Neaters.

●

Q. What do you get when you cross a Quidditch player with a scientist?
A. A beaker.

Q. What would you ride on for a game of indoor Quidditch?
A. A roomstick.

Q. What cleaning object appears only when you need it?
A. The Broom of Requirement.

●

Q. Where do Quidditch players keep their equipment?
A. In the broom closet.

Q. How do you play explosive Quidditch?
A. With a boomstick.

The Quidditch Pitch

Q. What do magical squirrels drink?
A. Nutterbeer.

Q. Did you know you can play Quidditch underground?
A. You have to use mole posts.

●

Say what you will, but Quidditch players are high-minded
    people.

●

Q. What has a handle and flies?
A. A Quidditch broom.

Q. What do wizards call baseball?
A. Dumb Quidditch.

●

Q. Why is summer the best time to play Quidditch?
A. Because the stands are full of fans.

●

Ron: I can tell you the score of a Quidditch game before it starts.
Hermione: Oh yeah?
Ron: Nothing to Nothing.

●

Q. Why did so many students want to date Oliver Wood?
A. Because he was a keeper!

●

Q. Where did Cedric go after he broke his leg playing Quidditch?
A. Madame Pomfrey's!

110

The Quidditch Pitch

Since Hufflepuffs are such great finders, they once fielded a
  Quidditch team that consisted entirely of Seekers!

•

**Q. What Hogwarts student would help you with your
  Quidditch skills?**
A. I think Oliver Wood.

•

Q. What type of broom goes so fast it could make you sick?
A. The Vomit.

Percy: Heard you skipped school for a Quidditch match.
Fred: That's a lie!
George: And we've got the candy from Honeydukes to
  prove it.

Q. What do you call a heavily injured Quidditch player?
A. A bad stitchuation.

Q. What kind of witches prefer croquet to Quidditch?
A. Wicket witches.

•

Cormac McLaggen was such a good friend.
What a keeper!

The Quidditch Pitch

Q. Why is it a good idea to get a good night's rest before a Quidditch match?

A. You can't sweep if you don't sleep!

•

Q. What made Madame Hooch hit the ceiling?

A. Trying to teach an indoor Quidditch lesson.

•

Q. What's the difference between Filch and Oliver Wood?

A. One is a creeper and the other is a keeper!

•

Q. How do Quidditch players always get points on the board?

A. With score-cery.

•

Q. How do broomsticks fly?

A. Through witch-fun thinking.

•

The weird thing about a Quidditch ball is that it *can* be beat!

Chapter 8

KNOCK-KNOCKTURN ALLEY

Knock-knock!
Who's there?
Hufflepuff.
Hufflepuff who?
I'll huffle, I'll puff, I'll blow your house down!

●

Knock-knock!
Who's there?
Theodore.
Theodore who?
Theodore Nott.
Not who?
No, Theodore Nott.
Huh?

Knock-Knockturn Alley

Knock-knock!
Who's there?
Freezing Charm.
Freezing Charm who?
Freezing Charms off if you go out there without a jacket!

●

Knock-knock!
Who's there?
Death Eater.
Death Eater who?
Death Eater sometimes, but he has to be polite.

●

Knock-knock!
Who's there?
Dobby.
Dobby who?
Dobby ridiculous!

●

Knock-knock!
Who's there?
Harry!
Harry who?
Harry up and let me in before this Whomping Willow gets me!

Knock-knock!
Who's there?
Albus.
Albus who?
Albus will be here soon, the Knight Bus, in fact!

Knock-knock!
Who's there?
Troll.
Troll who?
Troll-ing right along!

Knock-Knockturn Alley

Knock-knock!
Who's there?
Wand.
Wand who?
Wandering by and thought I'd say hi!

•

Knock-knock!
Who's there?
Quidditch.
Quidditch who?
Quidditch-ing that rash or it won't heal.

•

Knock-knock!
Who's there?
You-know-who.
You-know-who who?
What's so funny?

•

Knock-knock!
Who's there?
Wand.
Wand who?
Wand to let me in?

Knock-knock!
Who's there?
Alchemy.
Alchemy who?
Alchemy the test answers, what a guy!

Knock-knock!
Who's there?
Hogsmeade.
Hogsmeade who?
Hogsmeade a huge mess at the farm.

Knock-knock!
Who's there?
He-who-must-not-be-named.
He-who-must-not-be-named who?
What did I just say?!

Knock-knock!
Who's there?
Iguana.
Iguana who?
Iguana go watch the Quidditch match?

Knock-Knockturn Alley

Knock-knock!
Who's there?
Wizard with a Time-Turner.
Wizard with a Time-Turner who?
I have no idea what you mean.

•

Knock-knock!
Who's there?
Winky.
Winky who?
Winky so I know you haven't been petrified.

•

Knock-knock!
Who's there?
Wise.
Wise who?
Wizengamot is a waste of our time.

•

Knock-knock!
Who's there?
Flutterby Bush.
Flutterby Bush who?
Flutterby Bush and smell the roses.

Knock-knock!
Who's there?
Coffin.
Coffin who?
Coffin up a storm with all this dust on the Mirror of Erised!

Knock-knock!
Who's there?
Tent.
Tent who?
Escaped Tentacula!

Knock-knock!
Who's there?
Alecto.
Alecto who?
Alecto a new Minister of Magic!

Knock-knock!
Who's there?
Tonks.
Tonks who?
Tonks a million, pal!

Knock-Knockturn Alley

Knock-knock!
Who's there?
Annie.
Annie who?
Annie magi, watch us transform!

Knock-knock!
Who's there?
Auror.
Auror who?
Aurorble they hired Umbridge.

Knock-knock!
Who's there?
A wafer.
A wafer who?
Harry, Ron, and Hermione were a wafer so long in *Harry
Potter and the Deathly Hallows*.

•

Knock-knock!
Who's there?
Flitwick.
Flitwick who?
Don't Flitwick or the candle will die.

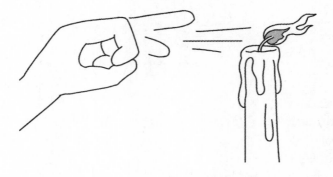

Knock-Knockturn Alley

Knock-knock!
Who's there?
Binns.
Binns who?
Bins are full, take out the trash.

Knock-knock!
Who's there?
Ivy.
Ivy who?
Ivy interested in seeing the Hufflepuff common room.

Knock-knock!
Who's there?
Severus.
Severus who?
Severus wondering if you wanted to have lunch?

●

Knock-knock!
Who's there?
Engine ears.
Engine ears who?
Engine ears drive the *Hogwarts Express*!

●

Knock-knock!
Who's there?
Diadem.
Diadem who?
Diadem magic powers I could do some amazing things!

●

Knock-knock!
Who's there?
Hoo.
Hoo who?
(The owl just puts down an envelope . . . and flies away!)

Knock-Knockturn Alley

Knock-knock!
Who's there?
Bullstrode.
Bullstrode who?
Bullstrode through and broke everything!

●

Knock-knock!
Who's there?
Paracelsus.
Paracelsus who?
Paracelsus some of those Acid Pops!

Knock-knock!
Who's there?
Sickle.
Sickle who?
Sickle you not letting me in when I come by!

Knock-knock!
Who's there?
Veela.
Veela who?
Veela weird attraction to this creature!

Knock-knock!
Who's there?
Kreacher.
Kreacher who?
Kreacher own destiny, Harry!

•

Knock-knock!
Who's there?
Ilvemorny.
Ilvermorny who?
Ilvermorny to hang out, and maybe the afternoon, too?

•

Knock-knock!
Who's there?
Harry.
Harry who?
Harry up or we'll be late for class!

•

Knock-knock!
Who's there?
Remus.
Remus who?
Remus visit soon!

Knock-knock!
Who's there?
Charms.
Charms who?
Charms tired from that Quidditch match!

•

Knock-knock!
Who's there?
Draco.
Draco who?
Draco my soda already, can I have some of yours?

•

Knock-knock!
Who's there?
Bloody Baron.
Bloody Baron who?
Bloody Baron the forest needs a bandage for his paw.

•

Knock-knock!
Who's there?
Shacklebolt.
Shacklebolt who?
Shacklebolt and lock the door when I leave!

128

Knock-Knockturn Alley

Knock-knock!
Who's there?
Fat Friar.
Fat Friar who?
Fat Friar doesn't work, how are we going to make this fried chicken?

Knock-knock!
Who's there?
Seeker.
Seeker who?
Seeker out after class.

Knock-knock!
Who's there?
Nox.
Didn't you already do that?

Knock-knock!
Who's there?
Mandrake.
Mandrake who?
Man, Drake's new album is great!

129

Knock-knock!
Who's There?
Woof!
Sirius?

Knock-knock!
Who's there?
Crabbe.
Crabbe who?
Crabbe you anything while I'm out?

Knock-knock!
Who's there?
Remembrall.
Remembrall who?
Remembrall the good times we had at Hogwarts?

Knock-knock!
Who's there?
Slytherin.
Slytherin who?
A basilisk is Slytherin through the forest. Do not engage!

Knock-Knockturn Alley

Knock-knock!
Who's there?
Dementor.
Dementor who?
Dementor trains an apprentice.

•

Knock-knock!
Who's there?
Floo.
Floo who?
Hey, don't cry.

•

Knock-knock!
Who's there?
Flamel.
Flamel who?
Flamel burn down the house, put it out!

•

Knock-knock!
Who's there?
Hedwig.
Hedwig who?
Yeah, that's what she says.

Knock-knock!
Who's there?
Quidditch.
Quidditch who?
Quidditch that coat? It's so warm outside!

Knock-knock!
Who's there?
Helga.
Helga who?
Helga with you to the Yule Ball if you ask him!

Knock-knock!
Who's there?
Rita.
Rita who?
Rita *The Quibbler* instead of *The Daily Prophet*!

Knock-knock!
Who's there?
Triwizard.
Triwizard who?
Triwizard accomplishes more than a no-try wizard.

Knock-Knockturn Alley

Knock-knock!
Who's there?
Toad.
Toad who?
Toadally not a good idea to drink a random potion!

Knock-knock!
Who's there?
Kettleburn.
Kettleburn who?
Kettleburn the house down if you don't watch it.

Knock-knock!
Who's there?
Lumos.
Lumos who?
Lumos and carrots sounds great!

Knock-knock!
Who's there?
Keeper.
Keeper who?
Keeper away from me!

Knock-knock!
Who's there?
Unicorn.
Unicorn who?
Unicorn outside or what?

Knock-knock!
Who's there?
Screwt.
Screwt who?
Screwt came loose in my chair, can you fix it?

Knock-Knockturn Alley

Knock-knock!
Who's there?
Veela.
Veela who?
Veela 'round sometime?

Knock-knock!
Who's there?
Gaunt.
Gaunt who?
Gaunt you see I'm busy?!

Knock-knock!
Who's there?
Who.
Who who?
Your owl impression is terrible!

Knock-knock!
Who's there?
Demiguise.
Demiguise who?
Demiguise are invisible, where did they go?

Knock-knock!
Who's there.
Erumpent.
Erumpent who?
Erumpent here to wrecked the place!

Knock-knock!
Who's there?
Doxy.
Doxy.
Doxy saw the hospital had a hard time treating his bite.

Knock-knock!
Who's there?
Occamy.
Occamy who?
Occamy door, I'd let you in!

Knock-knock!
Who's there?
Fairy.
Fairy who?
Fairy sure that Doxy bit me!

Knock-Knockturn Alley

Knock-knock!
Who's there?
Transfigured McGonagall.
Transfigured McGonagall who?
Meow.

•

Knock-knock!
Who's there?
Guy with a Time-Turner.
Guy with a Time-Turner who?
Knock-knock!
Who's there?
Guy with a Time-Turner.
Guy with a Time-Turner who?
Knock-knock!
Who's there?
Guy with a Time-Turner.
Guy with a Time-Turner who?
Sorry, it's broken because I used it too much.

Chapter 9

VOLDEMORT RETURNS

Q. Why did Voldemort chop up his shoe?
A. He wanted to leave behind pieces of his sole.

•

Q. What do you call Nagini in the Ministry of Magic?
A. A civil serpent.

•

Nagini is very hard to joke with.
You just can't pull her leg!

•

Q. What does Voldemort wear on his feet?
A. You-Know . . . shoes.

Q. What would you call a portrait of Voldemort?
A. He who must not be framed.

●

Q. What do you call a stinky dark wizard?
A. A Death Feeter.

Q. What dark wizards also cheat on their homework?
A. Death Cheaters.

Roses are red
Violets are blue
A flash of green light
Means goodbye to you.
—*a poem by Voldemort*

●

Q. What forms on horcruxes left alone for too long?
A. A horcrust.

●

Q. What do you call a rat that plays board games?
A. Scrabblers.

●

Ron missed Scabbers, even though he wasn't very mice.

●

Q. What did Ron say when Scabbers ran away?
A. "Rats!"

Q. Why did Nagini get sick?
A. She bit herself.

Q. Why was Nagini acting so weird?
A. She was off her head.

•

Q. Why did young Voldemort like board games?
A. He always rolled snake eyes.

•

Q. Why is Voldemort's face so flat, anyway?
A. He ran into platform 9 . . . and 10.

Q. Whom should you never borrow a book from?
A. Tom Riddle!

•

When Ginny Weasley grew up, she went into journalism . . .
  which she was introduced to by Tom Riddle.

•

Q. Why did Voldemort cover himself with protection spells?
A. Because he was "He who must not be maimed."

•

"Tom Marvolo Riddle" . . . And Other Anagrams for "I Am Lord Voldemort"
- Lord Earldom Vomit
- I Am Lord Old Mr. Out
- Mild Doormat Lover
- Dermal Drool Vomit
- Old Immortal Lover
- Milk Moor, Dad Lover
- Marmot Drool Devil

Q. What kind of architecture does Voldemort like best?
A. Dark art deco.

•

Q. If Tom Riddle is the heir of Slytherin, then who is Medusa?
A. The hair of Slytherin!

Q. What do you call an electrocuted Dark Lord?
A. Volt-demort.

Q. What happens when you combine fire with the Dark Lord?

A. Smolderingmort!

•

Q. Where do Death Eaters go to get their dark mark tattoos?

A. In the Dark Marking Lot.

•

Q. Did Voldemort have a good wand?

A. Sure, it was state of the dark art!

•

Q. But was it well made?

A. Yes, it was a work of dark art!

•

Q. What would you call a painting of Voldemort?

A. Dark art.

Q. What would you call a popsicle stick model of the Shrieking Shack?

A. Dark arts and crafts.

Q. What Hogwarts class will protect you from nerds?

A. Defense Against the Dork Arts.

•

Q. Why doesn't Voldemort wear glasses?

A. Nobody nose!

Q. How do Death Eaters freshen their breath?
A. With demint-os.

•

Q. Why did Death Eaters cross the road?
A. The Dark Lord told them to do it.

•

Q. Did you hear what happened to the killing curse Voldemort placed on baby Harry?
A. It rebounded . . . and killed his nose.

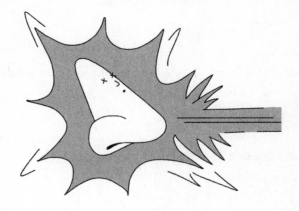

Voldemort Returns

Q. How could Voldemort have foiled Harry Potter forever?

A. He could have made the final horcrux his nose!

•

Q. Why did Voldemort lay low for so long?

A. He was embarrassed about his nose.

•

If you are what you eat then Voldemort . . . is a unicorn?

Q. Why can't they name a street after Voldemort?
A. Because nobody crosses Voldemort and lives!

•

Q. What do you call a fear of Lord Voldemort?
A. Logical!

•

Q. Why does Lord Voldemort sleep with a night light?
A. Because the dark is afraid of him.

Voldemort Returns

Q. How does Voldemort text a smiley face?
A. :)

•

Roses are red
Violets are blue
Mention my nose again
And I'll crucio you!
—*a poem by Voldemort*

•

Harry wears glasses
I left him for dead
Now he's got a scar
On the front of his head.
—*a poem by Voldemort*

•

Q. What's Voldemort's favorite kind of music?
A. Soul!

Q. What's Voldemort's favorite kind of fancy fish to eat?
A. Filet of sole.

•

Q. Where did Voldemort buy all his evil magic supplies?
A. At the Dark Arts Mart.

•

Q. What kind of chocolate does Voldemort like best?
A. Dark chocolate.

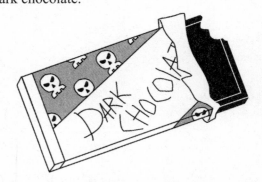

Q. Why did they bury Voldemort behind the big tree?
A. Because he was dead.

Chapter 10

THIS IS GETTING RIDDIKULUS!

Q. Who's the smartest owl who ever lived?

A. Owlbert Einstein.

Q. Why didn't the vampires like the wizard?

A. He was a mudblood.

Q. Did you hear that Winky won the lottery?

A. Now she's welfy.

Q. What do you get when you cross an insect with a non-magical person?

A. A buggle.

Q. What do you call a prison guard who makes sauerkraut?

A. A fermentor.

This is Getting Riddikulus!

Q. Who's the most magical and sweetest robot?
A. Bertie Bot.

Q. What's a wizard's favorite NBA team?
A. The Wizards.

Q. What's their other favorite NBA team?
A. The Magic.

Q. Who is a wizard's favorite basketball player?
A. Magic Johnson.

•

Q. Did you hear about the wizard who went broke?
A. He had knuttin'.

Q. Who should have directed the Harry Potter movies?
A. Steven Spellberg.

This is Getting Riddikulus!

Q. What do you call a non-magical person who likes to embrace?

A. A Huggle.

•

Q. What do you call a thieving house elf?

A. Robby.

Q. Did you hear that the boy who lived transformed into a cheetah?

A. He was a Hairy Spotter.

Harry Potter Characters . . . And Their License Plates
(If Wizards Drove Cars, That Is)

- DBLAGENT   Severus Snape
- HGSHEAD   Aberforth Dumbledore
- CHOSEN1   Harry Potter
- UKNOWWHO   Voldemort
- MRSLUPIN   Nymphadora Tonks
- MRTONKS   Remus Lupin
- WRMTAIL   Peter Pettigrew
- QUIBBLR   Xenophilius Lovegood
- FREEELF   Dobby
- WIZWHEEZ   Fred and George Weasley
- THRBROOMS   Madam Rosmerta
- HEMHEM   Dolores Umbridge
- VOLDLVR   Bellatrix Lestrange
- ARMCHAIR   Horace Slughorn
- SPEWGRL   Hermione Granger
- HEADBOY   Percy Weasley
- HISTORIAN   Bathilda Bagshot
- WANDMAN   Ollivander
- ILUVMUGGLS   Arthur Weasley

This is Getting Riddikulus!

Q. Did you hear they're making a TV show just about Hermione?

A. It's called *Granger Things*.

•

Q. In a ranking of most spooky creatures, where did Inferi fall?

A. Dead last.

•

Q. What's Hagrid's favorite Pixar movie?

A. *Monsters, Inc.*

•

Q. Why did the werewolf professor like roller coasters?

A. Because of all the "Lupin"!

•

A great prank for parent wizards to play on their kid: name them Wingardium Leviosa. Then when anyone says their name . . . they fly around!

Q. What should Jacob Kowalski have called his bakery?

A. "Fantastic Yeasts and Where to Find Them."

•

Tongue Twisters

- The gray Graphorns grabs great gray geese.
- Fwoopers swoop and sing fine songs
- A Billywig stings Willy Bings' sister, Wilma.
- There are many murtflaps on not many mudflats.
- It's nuts how Nifflers know knuts, not nuts.
- Ask ashwinders why ashwinders are harsh.
- Ted Tonk took two.
- Guess the best thestral.

•

Q. What would you get if you crossed Snape with a fairy tale?

A. The Half Blood Prince Charming.

•

Q. What owl can fix your yard up nice?

A. Hedgewig.

This is Getting Riddikulus!

Q. What kind of car does Hegwig drive?
A. An Owlsmobile.

•

Hedwig is so good at delivering letters, but hey, it's owl in a day's work.

•

Q. Did you hear that Hedwig had a party?
A. It was a regular hootenanny.

•

Q. What did Harry hope he didn't get for his 16ᵗʰ birthday?
A. A brand-new scar!

•

Q. What has 18 eyes, 17 ears, and lives in a burrow?
A. The Weasleys.

•

Vernon Dursley was mean, but he was at least good at his job. He kept the factory Grunnings.

Q. The owl post sure is a fun place to be.

A. They say it's a real hoot.

•

Q. What do you call a wizard that plays golf?

A. Harry Putter.

Q. What kind of bread makes good wizarding sandwiches?

A. Harry Pita.

This is Getting Riddikulus!

The Wizarding World Opposite Names Quiz
Name the character whose name we "opposite-ified."

1) Bald Digger
2) Smartwindow
3) Sunny Hate-Bad
4) Short-top
5) Beauty-Invite In

6) Silly White
7) Happy-Mouth
8) Important-Shrunk
9) Contribute
10) Bottom Real Hair

Answers:

1) Harry Potter
2) Dumbledore
3) Luna Lovegood
4) Longbottom
5) Hagrid
6) Sirius Black
7) Mad-Eye
8) Pettigrew
9) Filch
10) Hedwig

●

Q. Did you know that owls have their own social media network?

A. They don't use Twitter, they use Hooter.

●

Q. What would you get if you crossed Hermione with a centaur?

A. Hermio-neigh.

Q. What happens if you cross *The Quibbler* with a Chimaera?

A. Head-lion news!

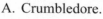

Q. What do you call a magic owl?

A. Hoot-Dini.

Q. What do you call a great wizard made of bread?

A. Crumbledore.

This is Getting Riddikulus!

**How to Tell Someone is a Muggle But They *Think*
They're a Wizard or a Witch**

- When they use a time-turner they just click a stopwatch and walk backwards really fast.
- Their magic wand is a breadstick.
- "Ariana Grande" is not a magic spell.
- When they say "expelliarmus," they just knock your wand out of your hand.
- When they grab something with magic, they say for it to work you have to close your eyes . . . and then they go over and get it.
- They say "lumos" but you know you saw them flip a light switch.
- When you ask them what house they were placed in, they say, "Magic House."

•

Q. What's Hedwig's favorite TV show?
A. *Doctor Who*.

•

Q. Who is a wizard's favorite band?
A. The Beedles.

Q. What do you call the place where Fluffy sleeps?
A. A barking lot!

Q. Who in the wizarding world will eat all your snacks?
A. Goblins!

•

Q. Was Regulus Black a good skateboarder?
A. Sure, he was totally R.A.B.!

This is Getting Riddikulus!

Real or Fake Harry Potter Character?

Of these thirty characters, only twenty are actually mentioned in the Harry Potter books. Can you spot the phonies?

1. Dedalus Diggle
2. Hepzibah Smith
3. Rundungus McVane
4. Walden Macnair
5. Priya Padhi
6. Felix Fickluss
7. Augustus Rookwood
8. Fletcher Rindongulung
9. Sturgis Podmore
10. Winston Bishop
11. Reg Cattermole
12. Nicholas Pelcher
13. Pius Thicknesse
14. Irma Pince
15. Albert Runcorn
16. Nigel Brimble
17. Griselda Marchbanks
18. Romilda Vane
19. Millicent Bulstrode
20. Terrence Trickleford
21. Piers Polkiss
22. Demelza Robins
23. Mafalda Hopkirk
24. Alecto Carrow
25. Emilia Hawltlung
26. Marcus Belby
27. Terry Boot
28. Wilkie Twycross
29. Penny Proclamo
30. Caractacus Burke

Answers: *The fakes are numbers 3, 5, 6, 8, 10, 12, 16, 20, 25, 29.*

Q. Did you hear about the wizard who was robbed by a No-Maj?

A. He was muggled!

•

The thing about Harry Potter puns is that they can Slytherin to any conversation.

•

Have you read the second Harry Potter book? It's petrifying!

•

Q. What's the difference between a bad apparation spell and a dinner you don't want to eat?

A. One has a splinch, the other has spinach.

•

Q. Who's the greatest magical baseball player of all time?
A. Ken Hippogriffy Jr.

•

Q. What would Kreacher most like to wear?
A. A nice new Kreach-shirt.

This is Getting Riddikulus!

Q. What kind of owls are the coldest?

A. Snowy owls.

•

Q. What do you call it when Hermione is angry, has her wand raised, and a spell ready to go?

A. Granger danger!

•

Q. What happened when the Whomping Willow sided with Voldemort?

A. It became a Bark Lord!

•

Q. What's a Potterhead's favorite Drake song?

A. "Started from the Longbottom now we're here"

•

Q. What do you get when you cross Gilderoy Lockhart with Remus Lupin?

A. Arrogant puppies.

You know you're a Potterhead if . . .

- You put glasses on your cat to see if maybe she could be Professor McGonagall in disguise.

- You did your career project at school on "auror."
- You get bummed out whenever the mail comes from some mail carrier and not an owl.
- You stare at pictures for hours, hoping to see somebody move.
- You've shouted "expelliarmus!" during a fight with a friend.
- You can explain the difference between a philosopher's stone and a sorcerer's stone.

This is Getting Riddikulus!

- You go camping and look around for the portkey.
- You go camping and expect your tent to be much larger on the inside.
- You go camping, see the ash left over from the last campfire and frantically look around for Ashwinder eggs.
- You've forgotten a key and tried "alohomora." (It didn't work.)
- When you've woken up in the middle of the night, you've tried "lumos!" to turn on the light.
- Whenever you see someone dressed weird, you assume they're a wizard.
- You look for the magic shops at the mall.
- You get disappointed when you look in a mirror and there's your reflection, and not your deepest desires.
- You try out Parseltongue at the zoo.
- For you, every weekend is a "Harry Potter weekend."
- You've asked an empty plate for what you want . . . and it didn't show up.
- When biting into a donut, you wonder for a second if it will turn you into a canary.
- You assume all tattoos are dark marks.
- You thought that that one song was called "What Does the Fawkes Say?"

- When it's foggy outside, you worry about Dementors.
- You got a pet lizard and named him Harry so you could say, "You're a lizard, Harry!"
- You wonder why you're friends with non-Potterheads.
- You're pretty sure you saw a thestral after every character death.
- You've tried to get your broomstick to "work."
- J.K. Rowling blocked you on Twitter because you asked too many questions!
- You send yourself Hogwarts letters in the mail.
- If you had to get a tattoo, you'd get the Deathly Hallows symbol.
- You've tried to get juice out of a jack-o-lantern.
- On school bus rides, you try to get singalongs of "Ninety-Nine Bottles of Butterbeer on the Wall" going.
- Pottermore isn't enough.
- You know that chocolate is the best medicine.
- You get bored with one-ball sports.
- You need more Harry Potter jokes!